# Elizabeth Bathory

# Edward Eaton

*A Play in 5 Scenes*

Published by
Dragonfly Publishing, Inc.

# Elizabeth Bathory
*Drama*

Paperback Edition
EAN 978-1-936381-45-6
ISBN 1-936381-45-1

eBook Edition
EAN 978-1-936381-46-3
ISBN 1-936381-46-X

Story Text ©2012 Edward Eaton
Cover Art ©2012 Dragonfly Publishing, Inc.
Dragonfly Logo ©2001 Terri L. Branson

*Published in the United States of America by*
Dragonfly Publishing, Inc.
Website: www.dragonflypubs.com

# TABLE OF CONTENTS

*This work is dedicated to my wife, Silviya,
and to my little man, Christopher.*

*Sine quibus non*

# *Acknowledgements*

*The playwright would like to thank
Richard Girardi and Brian Triber of Ubiquity
Stage for their support and encouragement.*

# CHARACTERS

ELIZABETH BATHORY: Hungarian Countess. She is arrogant, proud, imperious, beautiful, haughty, and alone. She is 54 years old, but in the flashbacks should look middle to early twenties, perhaps as young as thirteen or fourteen.

PRIEST: Young and fairly naïve Priest. He is ambitious, perhaps a bit recklessly so. Although well born, he is not particularly influential. If he succeeds at obtaining Elizabeth's confession/conversion, his career could take off. He is no older than his late twenties.

MOTHER: Elizabeth's mother. She is strong and accustomed to being obeyed. The director can decide her age. [Consider: Lady Capulet in *Romeo and Juliet* is 26.]

LADY IN WAITING: A Lady in Waiting.

MAID: A maid.

FERENC: A young, fierce warrior. He is a violent killer, but a tender lover. Women want him. Men want to be his friend.

STRANGER: Demonic and evil, he is creepily sexy.

THURZO: Early in the story, he is a young man only a few years older than Elizabeth. By the end, he is middle-aged. He is strong and proud, but not quite as heroic or attractive as Ferenc. Perhaps he has some issues with this.

GUARD: A guard.

SETTING: Hungary. The tower room in the Castle Cjesthe.

TIME: 1614

# SCENE I

---

*The lights come up to reveal the COUNTESS
ELIZABETH BATHORY huddled by the
fireplace, an old crone enveloped in a cloak.*

*We hear the screams of young women in torment.*

*We hear the wails of loss and mourning from
their families.*

*The voices fall silent.*

*There is the sound of a baby's crying.*

VOICE OF ELIZABETH
No! Not my boy! Not my baby!

VOICE OF MOTHER
Give it to me! Give me that child!

VOICE OF ELIZABETH
No!

VOICE OF MOTHER
Take it. Get rid of it. Expose it. Drown it. I do not care. Just get it out of
here.

VOICE OF ELIZABETH
No!

VOICE OF LADY IN WAITING
Have you seen Ferenc? He's so handsome. I wish I were you.

VOICE OF MOTHER
You are going to marry Ferenc. The guests are already arriving.

VOICE OF ELIZABETH
Never! I love—

VOICE OF MOTHER
He is not for you.

VOICE OF ELIZABETH
He loves me!

VOICE OF MOTHER
Whore!

VOICE OF ELIZABETH
But he—

VOICE OF STRANGER
Do you want to be old? Do you want to be lovely? Do you want to be Wanted? Desired?

VOICE OF THURZO
You, Elizabeth, are like a wild animal. I condemn you, Lady, to life-long imprisonment in your own castle.

> *All sound stops abruptly.*
>
> *A small hatch next to the large unused door opens and light bursts into the room.*
>
> *ELIZABETH hides her face.*
>
> *Someone looks through the hatch.*
>
> *It slams shut.*
>
> *There is the sound of arguing without.*

*Silence.*

*The hatch opens again.*

*ELIZABETH hisses at the light.*

*The hatch slams shut again.*

*Argument without.*

*Silence.*

*There are the sounds of ancient locks being broken and mortar being chipped away.*

*Eventually the door opens slowly.*

*Lights pours in.*

*A PRIEST enters the room. A GUARD without tries one last time, to persuade the PRIEST not to enter. The PRIEST insists. He comes all the way in, carrying his lantern and a sack. The GUARD slams the door shut.*

*The PRIEST is a young man. He clearly comes from a wealthy family. He bears himself as an intelligent, handsome, and confidant man. He is also nervous.*

*He looks around the room and takes stock of the situation. He looks at ELIZABETH with a mixture of disgust and apprehension.*

*He takes the sack and, careful not to get to close to ELIZABETH, places the bag next to her. He backs away from her and sits on the stool.*

> *ELIZABETH looks at the sack. She sniffs at it. Slowly she opens it and discovers food and some sort of flask. Animal-like, she tears into the food.*
>
> *The PRIEST looks on in disgust.*
>
> *He shudders and crosses himself.*

PRIEST
How one once so great could become like this.

God in heaven. Look down on this wretched creature and soften her heart.

Is this beast, this animal, feeding itself thus, really the remains of the Lady of Csejthe?

> *ELIZABETH stops eating and looks at the PRIEST for the first time.*

ELIZABETH
Bastard.

> *The PRIEST crosses himself.*

ELIZABETH
Get out. Bastard.

> *ELIZABETH continues to feed herself.*

PRIEST
So, you are the ancient witch who lives in the tower?

Or is it 'vampire'?

I have heard so many stories, I really can't keep them straight.

You don't look nearly so frightening as you should. Little more than a bedtime story told to frighten naughty children. "Behave yourself, or we'll feed you to the Countess Elizabeth."

Ha, ha.

*Pause.*

So. You are the great and powerful Countess Elizabeth Bathory.

ELIZABETH
I was.

PRIEST
It speaks.

I'm sure you've made you family proud of you.

ELIZABETH
What does it matter to you, Priest?

PRIEST
I remember when the king learned what you'd been up to.

How many was it? Over 600?

Is that right? That's what I heard. But the numbers get confused in the telling.

One would have been too many, I think.

The king still sometimes talks about putting you out of your misery. Some kindling. One torch. And poof! The rotting bones go up in smoke and no more Countess. We could have a carnival, with your immolation as the main attraction.

Ha, ha.

*Pause.*

I've seen burnings. You know, it's the smoke that actually kills you. Most of the time. Saw one man burn once who caught a bad wind. His sins must have been great. The smoke blew away from him. It took him four hours to die.

They said you could hear his screams two towns over. I believe it. It was quite unnerving.

But there are those of us who have convinced the king that there is no way to guarantee a good wind. And four hours is not nearly enough time. Not nearly enough time.

No matter. You can't live for too long shut up in here. How you've lived for three years is beyond me.

Does my light burn your eyes? Where are my manners? Let me move it closer to you. Better?

Don't worry, I shan't let it burn you, witch.

*Pause.*

What a glorious domain you have here, Countess.

How lovely. You've clearly worked hard on it.

And where are your subjects? Or did you kill all the rats and mice?

Did you bathe in their blood?

Did you eat their flesh?

Did you make love to them?

Or are there some things too depraved even for you?

*Long pause.*

ELIZABETH
Please go.

> *Long pause.*
>
> *The PRIEST turns and goes.*
>
> *Time passes. The PRIEST returns with a small amount of food. ELIZABETH ignores the PRIEST but wolfs down the food and drinks deeply of whatever liquid he brought her.*

ELIZABETH
Are you still here?

PRIEST
It speaks again! I was hurt; I thought you'd forgotten me.

ELIZABETH
I thought you were a bad dream.

PRIEST
I wish I were. But I'm sure you've had enough of those these past years.

> *Pause.*

Have you?

What dreams do you have?

What screams do you hear?

What faces come to you in the night?

What haunts you, witch?

> *ELIZABETH turns away and retreats to her earlier place. The PRIEST turns to go.*

*Time passes.*

*The PRIEST squats and watches ELIZABETH. He holds out the food and makes her come and take it from his hands. As she is just about to snatch it, he pulls it away.*

*Pause.*

ELIZABETH
Thank you.

*The PRIEST gives her this food and she eats it a little more delicately than she had the earlier times.*

ELIZABETH
*[After a time]*
Flowers.

PRIEST
Flowers? What? Where?

ELIZABETH
Flowers.

I see flowers.

PRIEST
I see no flowers, old woman. What are you talking about?

ELIZABETH
I see flowers.

In here. Out there.

I do not dream of walls and dust, Priest.

Your nightmares are my reality. My nightmares are your dreams.

When I was a child, my governesses would give me lessons in my mother's gardens. I would escape from them and play among the trees and wade in the pools.

And then here. I used to have such lovely gardens. And so many lovely flowers. I could go there to escape the court and skip barefoot along the grassy paths. Make love among the flowers.

I must have had fifty kinds of roses alone. They were always my favorite. I used to sleep on pillows filled with their petals.

My husband's first gift to me, even before I met him, was a wagon filled with the whitest of roses. So white they blinded me. I thought I'd never see anything so beautiful.

Then I got his second gift…after we were married.

But there are some things the sensitive ears of a priest could never understand.

PRIEST
Whore.

ELIZABETH
He was my husband.

As for the others…I always gave myself quite freely.

But I was thinking of my flowers.

> *Offstage, faintly, we hear the sound of young people playing in a garden.*

So lovely under the sun as they caught its beams and held them to brighten even the darkest moonless night.

When I close my eyes, Priest, I see my flowers. I see my garden.

PRIEST
And it truly is lovely. I saw it when I came in.

ELIZABETH
No matter. I do not care what became of it. I cannot see it. It does not exist for me.

PRIEST
But the garden is just outside your window. If you could reach out, you could touch the ivy that grows along the wall. If you tried, you could probably smell the roses.

ELIZABETH
When I was first here, I tried to remove the bricks.

All I did was tear my hands.

But the memory is enough.

Now leave me.

You have had your time to gawk.

I am old and tired. I have become used to my solitude. I have no need for company.

PRIEST
I am not here for a visit, witch.

I did not come to keep you company.

You will have plenty of company in hell.

ELIZABETH
If my only companions on earth are to be priests, I'd much prefer hell.

PRIEST
And soon enough, God be willing, you will be there.

ELIZABETH
God will do me no favors. He never has before.

PRIEST
Hasn't He?

Hasn't He?

Who gave you family?

Who gave you position?

You come from one of the great families in Hungary. Was that just luck? Was God's will, may he be praised.

Was God made you beautiful.

Was God made you rich.

But you, in your vanity and pride, sought to compete with God's gifts.

You fell from His grace and sought diabolical means to fight His will.

Witchcraft is a grievous sin, lady.

If it were up to me, you would die unshriven. But…your family still has influence.

My Archbishop has commanded that I come and ask for your confession.

*ELIZABETH spits.*

ELIZABETH
I do not serve Rome.

I will not serve Rome.

PRIEST
Your own kind have abandoned you.

Rome might very well be your only hope.

Soften your heart and God's mercy might be—

ELIZABETH
No deathbed conversion for me, Priest.

Was a papist king locked me in here.

*Pause.*

So, who are you, boy?

You are wealthy, well fed, well kept. You're not a local boy. You're not a parish priest.

You are a courtier, I'd guess. Hmm.

My conversion would certainly be an asset to your career.

Ah!

The truth?

Or is it?

Are you merely some lonely priest who wishes to listen to a life he cannot live?

A eunuch who wishes to learn about sensuality?

A hermit who wishes to dance in the halls of the great?

Why do you want to learn of my little sins?

PRIEST
I am only here...the Archbishop wants, wishes...I hope to save your soul.

ELIZABETH
Save your own soul, Priest.

No! Do not speak.

For three years I have been locked in this room this one small room. In my own castle. I have no servants. No companions. Only the rats.

Only the vermin.

The only light is out of reach.

I do not even wish to talk about the food. Thank you, by the way.

But, perhaps the cruelest trick of all is that the only one to speak to me for three years is a Bible thumping priest trying to balance his own accounts.

Will conversion bring me friends?

Will confession bring me my gardens? My roses?

Will they clear these windows and allow the sun inside again?

PRIEST
No.

But they will allow the Son of God inside again.

ELIZABETH
The hell with the Son of God.

PRIEST
Blasphemy.

ELIZABETH
Only blasphemy? I must be slipping in my dotage.

If my crimes were so great, why am I still alive?

Why not murder me now and allow your God to punish me.

PRIEST
Your punishment is just.

You sought immortality? Then live forever here. Eternity will be very lonely, Lady.

> *The PRIEST turns to go.*

> *Time changes.*

> *The PRIEST returns.*

Did you know that the guards have orders to replace your mirror should you ever break it. The king wants you to be able to watch yourself grow old and wither.

I have seen portraits of you in your youth. You certainly were lovely.

What an irony to see such great beauty ravaged by time and neglect.

Has it been fun being an old crone?

ELIZABETH
*[Laughs]*
You don't know the half of it, Priest.

> *Pause.*

Let me show you the old crone I have become.

PRIEST
Keep back, witch.

*ELIZABETH casts off her cloak. Underneath, she is nearly naked. She is quite lovely. Although she is 54, she looks much, much younger. She should be pretty, beautiful, and sexy. Her looks should denote a great personal charisma and charm. Her eyes are intelligent. She should glow with freshness. Her smile should melt the hardest of hearts. She should be confident with her beauty, even a little arrogant about it. There should also be a certain coldness to her.*

PRIEST
Holy Mary, Mother of God....

ELIZABETH
Keep your Holy Maries to yourself, priest. Virginity was always overrated.

*The PRIEST flees.*

*Time Changes.*

*The PRIEST returns. ELIZABETH is still exposed. She rises as the PRIEST enters and starts for him.*

PRIEST
Stand away!

ELIZABETH
Look at me, Priest.

Look at me.

Look at the old crone that I have become.

Look at my wrinkled skin and sagging breasts.

Look at my graying hair and sunken cheeks.

Look at what time has done to me.

Look at what my sins have turned me into.

Did they not tell you?

My jailers...they have always known.

I was not locked in here to grow old. Were I a faded crone, solitude would be a blessing.

When I look in the mirror, I see this body. I see this face.

Do you think any man could damn me?

Do you like what you see, Priest?

PRIEST
Lord Christ, protect me and deliver me from evil.

ELIZABETH
He does not come here, Priest. You are on your own.

Of course, you could always run.

Leave this place and crawl back to your archbishop!

What would you tell him?

Would he believe you?

Do you?

Do you trust your eyes? Or would you like to touch me? To feel my skin? My flesh?

Have you ever touched a woman before?
How can you judge my sins without knowing how they feel.

I know exactly how lovely I was. I know exactly the hideous crone I have become.

We all do.

That's part of our charm. Isn't it?

Go ahead. Look. Touch. Want. There's nothing wrong in that. That's why they're here.

That's why you're here. You just won't admit it.

PRIEST
Clothe yourself!

ELIZABETH
Why should I clothe myself? I feel so free naked. Nothing restricts me. Nothing holds me back.

PRIEST
Please. Clothe yourself.

ELIZABETH
Manners. I'm impressed.

But not in that old rag. I don't think so. Not when I have company for the first time in so long.

> *She goes to the chest and opens it. She begins to remove several beautiful cloaks.*

Sometimes I take my old clothes from the trunk and try them on in front of the mirror.

I can remember how men looked at me.

Women too. Don't you believe that, Priest? Does that shock you? I can remember being touched and caressed.

I can see my lovers' faces.

I can feel their fingers against my skin. The touch of their lips on my breasts. Mouths kissing me. Bodies crushed against me.

The strength of their—

Now there are only my fingers. My mouth.

PRIEST
Clothe yourself!

ELIZABETH
Which one should I wear?

PRIEST
I do not care.

ELIZABETH
You must choose, Priest.

I am not ashamed of my body. Why are you afraid of what your God gave me?

Why should I hide my light under a bushel?

PRIEST
[Desperately]
That one!

ELIZABETH
The white one?

PRIEST
Yes!

*ELIZABETH hands the white one to the PRIEST and places the others back in the trunk. She walks to the PRIEST and stands with her arms spread, waiting for him to dress her.*

*There is a pause, for however long, while the PRIEST decides what to do. Eventually, he tentatively and carefully places the cloak on her shoulders.*

# SCENE II

ELIZABETH
Thank you.

And, well chosen.

My husband gave this to me on the day we were married. I wore it to the bridal chamber.

The color wasn't appropriate, but he didn't know that.

See, I look quite lovely in it.

What a wedding it was. It was the event of the year. The joining of two great families, though mine was the better of the two.

LADY IN WAITING (V.O.)
Have you seen Ferenc?

Have you?

He's so handsome. I wish I were you.

And so important.

Did you know that the Emperor might be coming?

The Emperor himself!

ELIZABETH
But he was unable to. That upset my mother no end. But he did send an ambassador.

The gifts.

The balls. I had never danced so much in my life. So many young men begging for the chance to touch me before...before my husband did.

Such lovely music!

Such pretty dresses!

For days before the ceremony we danced and laughed and danced even more.

> *She dances as if she's in a ballroom surrounded by beaux.*

LADY IN WAITING (V.O.)
They say he's on his way. He'll be here soon.

Don't look so glum. He's coming.

Come and dance some more. Everyone is waiting.

ELIZABETH
I was the center of it all. I was no longer just some extra daughter waiting to be married off. I was the princess. I was the one everyone loved. Envied. It was I. Young. Beautiful. Wanted. Adored.

LADY IN WAITING (V.O.)
He has sent a messenger. He'll be here any day now. Don't be sad. I'm sure he'll make it up to you.

PRIEST
Why were you sad?

ELIZABETH
And, believe it or not, Priest, relatively innocent.

*When ELIZABETH is speaking with and interacting with people from her past, they should be emotionally connecting, but physically separated and not actually acting together. There could also be some technical way of establishing the different timelines (use of light or something).*

MOTHER
Innocent. Don't pretend to be so innocent.

Don't be so coy.

You had just better hope that you fool Ferenc. But I know what you are.

Don't worry. Even if he is unable to show, you wouldn't be the first girl married by proxy.

ELIZABETH
I didn't mean—

MOTHER
I know what you meant, girl. I know exactly what you meant.

Well, he's not coming. Get that thought out of your head.

Don't try those sad eyes on me, slut.

ELIZABETH
Please.

I want to marry—

MOTHER
Never. Not while I live.

You are marrying the Count Ferenc. That is the end of it.

The other — that was a mistake.

ELIZABETH
How can you say that?

MOTHER
Had I been here—

ELIZABETH
Jealous, Mother? Is that why I'm marrying Ferenc? Because you are jealous of your own daughter?

How pathetic!

MOTHER
Don't speak to me in that tone of voice, girl.

Ferenc is a great man.

ELIZABETH
He's a butcher.

MOTHER
This 'butcher' is one of our greatest generals. He's rich. Powerful.

ELIZABETH
I'll never be a wife to him.

MOTHER
You will be whatever he wants you to be, girl. What do you think you are? Know your place. You will belong to him.

Look, little girl.

We are a great family. But we are no longer as rich as we once were. Ferenc is rich, powerful. We both stand to gain so much from this marriage.

You have cousins who need advancement.

We need money.

You will get that for us.

Girl, this is your job. No one raises daughters to leech off the family fortune. You are brought into this life to be married off. To make a man happy. To help better us.

Don't be so selfish.

ELIZABETH
It's not fair.

MOTHER
Who said anything about being fair?

I didn't know your father before we were married. I barely knew who he was. I hardly spoke the same language.

But I understood what was expected of me. I understood my duty.

And the result was fine. Your father and I have had a happy marriage. For years.

Do your duty by Ferenc, and you will be happy. I want you to be happy. I do.

ELIZABETH
But I don't want to marry that filthy butcher. I want a prince. Someone to love me and whom I love.

MOTHER
You are being naive, girl.

It is arranged. The guests have arrived. That's the end of it.


Everything is arranged. I will not be embarrassed because of some spoiled brat. Daughter or no daughter.

But do as you like.

It is your choice. We are not barbarians. Just say 'no' during the ceremony.

We can't force you.

If you say no, however, then you will be out.

I shan't lose any sleep. I shan't miss a meal.

You are certainly pretty enough. You could probably survive well enough for a few years. But no prince, great or small, will marry an outcast.

But remember, aging wives are respectable. Aging whores starve.

But, as I said, it is your choice.

ELIZABETH
I couldn't really starve, now, could I?

Could you see me hungry? Poor? Unwanted?

I know it happens to some people. I'm told it's worse to be poor having been rich than always having been poor.

I could not allow that to happen to me.

I'd figure out a way to get what I wanted. Duty or no.

Married or no, I would not spend my life as chattel.

PRIEST
Who did you want to marry?


ELIZABETH
What?

Oh.

Just pre-wedding jitters, Priest.

The wedding almost didn't happen.

Ferenc was a warrior, as you know. He had been away killing Turks, or something like that, just before the wedding. He almost didn't make it in time.

He was so late that some guests were leaving when he came in.

> *FERENC bursts in. He is tall, dark, gorgeous, heroic. He is almost ideally male. He is dressed for killing. He is covered in blood. He looks like a young man in his early 20s.*
>
> *In the distance, we can hear the soft ringing of wedding bells.*

I knew, as soon as I saw him, that I wanted him. But I also hated him.

Was I to be chattel? However much a man he was, might be, I could not be his property. I could not love him as I....

I played my part during the ceremony. I said the words in a haze. I remember little except that someone said I was wife. Ferenc lifted my veil and....

> *FERENC goes through the motions of lifting her veil and kissing her gently. She feels his caress.*

I held my tongue at the reception. And later was escorted by giggling maids to the bridal chamber.

I felt like an object. The guests standing outside leering at me. Knowing what I would be doing with my drunken warrior husband.

Was this duty? To be paraded to my husband's bed. For our first time to be the subject for drunken carousing and public scrutiny.

I was no fool. I knew exactly what to expect. I'd heard too many stories of drunken fumbling. I'd stood outside too many doors to not know of being hammered into. Of sleeping under dead weight after he'd passed out from thirty seconds' exertion.

Don't be so shocked, Priest. I, and all women, are aware that husbands are notoriously...expeditious — is that the word? — lovers. Why do you think we do not care that our husbands take mistresses? Why do you think so many children don't look like their fathers.

So I prepared myself.

> *ELIZABETH stands, offering herself coldly. FERENC looks at her for a moment. He smiles. Gently, he motions for her to sit. He presents himself to her.*

FERENC
Leave off the warfare. That is who I am, but it is not all of me.

Call me warrior. But also call me man, husband, lover.

Imagine we are simple folk, living deep in the forest. No one else is there. No one. We reap. We sew. We tend our flocks. That is our life. That is our life. We fight the rains. The bitter winters. The parching droughts.

But, together, we can endure the work and the solitude. Together we can stand against any hardship.

Come dance with me. Come be with me under the starry sky. Smile to the moon and wave to the clouds. For they are our roof. Only they can see us, and they share in our new-found love.

Imagine we live among the trees. Dancing on the leaves. Playing with the beasts. Alone we play and hunt. We bathe in the purest of streams and make love in the glades.

Come dance with me. Leap with me among the trees. Play with the deer and sing to the birds. For they are our family.

Fear me not, for I love you. With me you shall come to no harm. My only fear is that my love will scare you, for you have never met its like before. Come love me. Trust me. For all that I am, all that I can, all that I will is yours.

Come dance with me. Give me your youth. I shall give you my strength. For we belong to each other.

> *Although ELIZABETH tries to resist FERENC, she is gradually drawn in by his words. FERENC makes his way to the bed.*

ELIZABETH
Do you know what it is like, Priest? Can you know?

Can you understand the raw power of a man?

Maybe a priest would.

I had never known such pleasure. It would only be a long time after his death that anything I would experience would even be half so wonderful.

And my beautiful Ferenc. Would anyone have thought that any one so violent — a killer — could love me so gently.

> *FERENC embraces his wife, picks up his sword and charges off.*

The danger of being married to a soldier is that they spend most of their time killing rather than making love.

My darling was away so very often.

But he was one of the best. The Black Knight of Hungary!

Even his enemies called him that.
But when he would return...then he would be all mine.

But you don't want the details, do you, Priest?

And so the years passed.

My darling, Ferenc away most of the year killing whoever it was that he killed. I never really cared to know whom.

And for a few precious weeks each year he would return to me.

And I would be so happy. For a time.

I was my own mistress.

I cast aside my mother and her family with little more than a pittance.

They kept the dowry. No matter. I had this beautiful castle. My courtiers. My servants.

Yet….

I began to grow older.

PRIEST
It happens to all of us. It is no great mystery. It is God's plan.

ELIZABETH
It was not mine.

I had done my duty. I was lucky to find so loving a husband. But my sacrifices to duty owed me more.

I was no longer the innocent child that he'd married.

I was no longer the young woman that he'd held in his arms.

I—I could find gray in my hair.

I—I could see wrinkles in the mirror.

My breasts were no longer so firm, my waist no longer so thin.

I was hideous.

FERENC
Don't be ridiculous.

I love you old or young.

I love every wrinkle. Every gray hair.

I love every moment that I am with you.

The youth and beauty that I love will be with you however old you are.
And so will I.

ELIZABETH
But, of course, I didn't believe that.

When he would be away fighting, I would try every diet, every berry,
every drug, every salve that the locals swore would keep me young.

And he would be away fighting.

I tightened my corset and painted my face.

And he would be away fighting.

I made myself sick from worry.

And he would be away fighting.

My lover was lost to me, even though he tried to tell me it wasn't so.

I was alone. Surrounded by courtiers and visitors, servants...I was alone.
I was lonely.

*A MAID is revealed as if she is brushing hair.*

With my husband I was loved and caressed. Without him I was obeyed.

My husband was a lover. I couldn't choose any of these men as lovers. I would have been ruined. They would have been dead.

I had no pleasure.

I had nothing.

And then…I learned something.

A silly maid, while brushing my hair, pricked me with a comb.

Bitch!

*The MAID reacts as if being slapped.*

Something I'd only heard about whispered out of sight.

I saw the fear in her eyes. The knowledge that if I spoke the word, she would be cast out, maybe killed.

The fear.

It was….

Was…so….

And her need to please me.

I slapped her again. Then I touched her red face. She shivered under my touch.

So I hit her again.

She began to cry, the silly girl. To cry!

The power I had to make this girl cry. To make her drop to her knees with tears streaming from her eyes.

They were salty, the tears. Salty just like mine. Just like mine.

And she became just like a puppet. Her hands moving where I commanded. Her body moving like I wanted.

As a wife, my duty was to please my husband.

As a slave, her duty was to please me.

A pleasure I never thought to feel.

I'd never thought of this. Oh, I know men do. It just never occurred to me that I could. To have such power. To be free to care only for my own pleasure.

PRIEST
I do not want to hear this.

To have violated the marriage bed would be enough. But through this depravity. This infamy.

ELIZABETH
Why depraved?

Why infamous?

Men take lovers. Why not women? I am Countess. I am Sovereign. It was my right. It is my right.

And the fear in that young girl's eyes was so…exciting.

Such a soft and smooth body. So safe.

Cleaned up, she might almost have been mistaken for a lady.

Almost.
Don't priests and monks do the same? Don't soldiers.

Why is pleasure a sin?

> *Throughout the previous, ELIZABETH has been building to a climax. At the same time, FERENC has been fighting for his life against some sort of great foe.*

PRIEST
Should God be willing to forgive your other sins, he will surely punish you for this.

> *As ELIZABETH approaches climax, FERENC is beaten and killed.*

> *ELIZABETH's screams at climax are not only those of pleasure, but those of the deepest pain and greatest loss as her husband dies.*

# SCENE III

---

ELIZABETH
He did.

He did.

He punished me.

He put me through hell.

Damn you.

Damn you and all your kind.

Damn you all.

I deny you all.

No God would do this to anyone.

Not to me.

I am the Countess Elizabeth Bathory.

My Darling Ferenc.

My husband.

Give him back to me.

Give me my love, damn you.

Damn you.

You owe me.

Give me back my husband.


PRIEST
That I cannot do. Even if I would I can...not!

*Long pause.*

ELIZABETH
I had nothing left.

I was alone.

*Long pause.*

PRIEST
You had friends. Family. Servants.

*Long pause.*

ELIZABETH
Friends? Pshaw!

What friends?

Would my friends have allowed me to stay here for so long?

No. There were no friends.

I had servants and courtiers. What use are they but to be used. I cannot love a slave. I cannot love a parasite.

For almost thirty years I had lived and loved for one man only. Now he was gone.

He was my friend. My companion. My lover.

He would hold me in the night.

For all my faults, for all my fading beauty, he loved me.

What was left for me now?

Nothing.

To be married off to an ancient widower, or someone's simple cousin.

I was used to the great life: months in Vienna at the Imperial Court, the gardens, the flowers, the wealth, the power.

How could I go from the wife of the Hero of Hungary, to some forgotten dowager? Old. Alone.

*Enter MOTHER.*

MOTHER
My poor child. My poor girl.

Don't be so suspicious.

I'm here for you. To comfort you in your grief. It's your mother's place to be here in your time of grief.

You're my daughter.

I know we've had our problems. My dear girl, mothers and children always fight. That is the way of things. It's part of being a child. It's part of being a mother.

But you're not a child any more. You're a woman who has lost her husband. And to spend your time locked away in this dreadful castle will only serve to make your grief all the worse.

I want to help you. You're my daughter and I love you.

There, there child. I will help you through it. I will always be here for you. There, there.

So I was right, in the end, wasn't I?

You will have to trust me again.

I will find you an even better husband.

Of course, we will wait for a suitable period.

You are still fairly attractive, considering your age. Too old to bear children, but with Ferenc's money, we should be able to do just fine by you.

ELIZABETH
No!

MOTHER
Don't be touchy, dear.

What else have you to do?

And don't worry about your age; it is the way of things.

You should really have given Ferenc a child. If you had a child, you could raise him, advise him.

But you don't have that luxury.

Do you really think that I could allow you to waste away in self-imposed exile.

You can help the family so much.

ELIZABETH
I don't want to help....

MOTHER
Of course you do.

You have been given so much; it is your turn to give in return.

ELIZABETH
Get out.

MOTHER
You don't mean that.

ELIZABETH
Get out!

This is my home. Mine. I am the Countess Elizabeth Bathory. I owe you nothing.

Get out!

MOTHER
You are an ungrateful bitch. A whore if I remember correctly.

ELIZABETH
Who are you to speak that way to me?

MOTHER
Someday you will need the family. A remote widow of your age will never have any influence or power.

*MOTHER exits.*

ELIZABETH
What else could I do?

PRIEST
Honor thy father and thy mother....

ELIZABETH
And why is that?

PRIEST
It is in the Holy Scriptures.

ELIZABETH
Do you really believe everything you read? There's a pity. All books have
been written by men. They can all be called to question.

Just because that old woman bore me, should I then pay for it all my life?
I didn't ask to be born. None of us did.

Should we honor the parents who beat us, who rape us, who steal from
us?

I think not.

I grew up the way she wanted. I dressed the way she wanted. I married
the way she wanted.

I was dutiful, and never caused a scandal.

But now I was rich.

It certainly was not like she was in danger of living on the streets.

No! Quite the opposite. There were innumerable cousins and nephews to
take her in. She could cry about her ingrate child, and they would pity
her. She'd have no pity here. She would have no love here.

And I. I would not allow myself to be treated as chattel. I had done my
duty. Nevermore.

*Pause.*

But she was right. Who had any need for an aging widow? With my
husband alive I had power and influence. But with him dead, I was just
an aging crone. The only value I had was that I could afford to marry
well.

But then, my only attraction would be money. No one could love me again. Not as I'd been loved before.

If only I'd known at twenty what I knew at forty.

That's something they don't tell women. Something they don't teach us. They let us learn, all right. But by then, it's too late.

And there I was. I knew. But I was old and alone.

*Pause.*

Why do you come here, Priest?

PRIEST
I told you.

ELIZABETH
To save my soul.

Why you? Why were you chosen?

PRIEST
My reasons for being here have nothing to do with—

ELIZABETH
They have everything to do with it.

PRIEST
I am here to hear your confession.

ELIZABETH
And I would hear yours.

> *Long pause. The Priest considers her request. He rises to leave.*
>
> *Time Changes.*

Well?

*Long pause.*

PRIEST
When I was a boy, my career in the cloth was decided. I am a younger son. There was not enough land for me. And I am not the warrior, as you can see.

> *ELIZABETH reaches out and grabs his arm to feel it. The PRIEST reacts back.*

Please, Lady.

ELIZABETH
I will not bite you, boy.

See. My teeth are dull. I'm not as young as I once was.

*Pause.*

PRIEST
Nor do I have the temperament of a butcher.

But I was always clever, so I was favored by His Eminence. Even though I was not yet ordained, I became something of a secretary to him. In that function, I went with him to pay court to the Emperor.

You were there.

ELIZABETH
That must have been fifteen years ago. I remember speaking to your Archbishop.

PRIEST
That was I with him. Do you remember?

ELIZABETH
Why should I remember some brat not yet in his teens?

Unlike your Archbishop, pre-pubescence does not excite me.

*Pause.*

PRIEST
I remember you.

You were like an angel.

I have met many ladies in my life, great and mean, beautiful and hideous.

You stood out.

What doubts I had of God's plan were washed away.

I saw an angel that day. Someone touched by God's Grace.

ELIZABETH
I had long since fallen from your God's grace.

PRIEST
Perhaps.

When I heard what you had done, I wept.

As Lucifer had fallen, so had you.

And as God awaits Lucifer's return, I prayed for yours.

How could someone as beautiful as you be so evil?

ELIZABETH
You think I'm beautiful?

PRIEST
You know you are.

ELIZABETH
I need to hear you say it.

PRIEST
Yes!

*ELIZABETH weeps.*

*Enter the STRANGER.*

STRANGER
Why is someone as beautiful as you so sad?

ELIZABETH
Beauty, bah!

My old bones will rest here to whither and die.

STRANGER
That is no future for one as lovely as you.

ELIZABETH
Are you trying to be funny, blind man?

STRANGER
I am not blind, lady. Indeed, I see what many do not.

ELIZABETH
What do you see?

STRANGER
I see what you once were.

I see a beautiful young woman, flushed with youth. Waiting the return of her new husband.

ELIZABETH
That was a long time ago.

STRANGER
No so long ago.

ELIZABETH
That girl is dead. I am what remains.

STRANGER
She is not dead, my lovely. She is still here.

Her heart beats in this breast. These feet still long to dance in the garden. These lips still wait to be kissed. This body still waits to be filled.

ELIZABETH
No, please.

STRANGER
Isn't this how Ferenc once touched you. How he kissed you.

ELIZABETH
Please.

My husband is dead. Let me die.

STRANGER
Never.

You're not so old that you can't enjoy your youth — that I cannot enjoy your youth.

ELIZABETH
The aged cannot youthen. That is the way of creation.

STRANGER
Maybe. But are you sure that your God's creation is the only one?

You are only old because you have aged. Your God allows this. Your God puts you on the earth to age and die.

Did your husband age?

ELIZABETH
You know he didn't.

STRANGER
That is because of the blood of his enemies.

ELIZABETH
I am not a man. I have no enemies to kill.

STRANGER
Is that so?

Men are fighters. Women are lovers. Men live through their violence. Women live through beauty and youth.

Do you want to be old?

Do you want to fade and wither?

Do you want the pity of the young?

Do you want their sniggers and jokes?

Do you want to need their help?

Do you want to be an invalid?

Do you want everyone waiting for you
to dry up and die?

Do you want to be young again? To be fresh? Lovely? Wanted? Desired?

> *The STRANGER brings out the MAID.*

Why not start with her? She killed your husband, after all.

Men have known it for years. The power of your enemy's blood and heart. That is what gives them power. That is what helps them maintain their youth.

But for women, it is different. Women's power comes from their beauty and youth. The most powerful women are young. Are in their twenties. For that is when they can control men. You produce heirs and you have power. You excite men's bodies and you have power. But you are too stupid so young to use your power except for petty reasons, pretty baubles, protestations of love, caresses, kisses.

Is that all you want? Trinkets and words.

When your husband was alive, men bowed and scraped the floor before you. Because Ferenc valued you and listened to you. You were lucky.

Now you have age, experience and wisdom. Now you are the woman you should have been when you first married. You could make poor men princes, kings, emperors, and emperors gods.

But who wants you now. Does your body excite? Does your charm move?

What can she do? This peasant girl? She is stupid, slow and will never have any value to anyone. Her innocence wasted on a toothless moron. Her virginity traded for a few cattle and a bail of hay. Her children to be born, raised, and die mindless and unloved.

But for a few years, she will be young. She will be beautiful.

Her body belongs to you. Why not take her beauty, her innocence. They belong to you too.

Do you remember what is was like to be young? Do you remember the gaze of men? Their touch? Their caresses?

Do you want them to pursue you? To want you? To need you? Or would you prefer lovers who merely fear you.

Do you want power and love? Or do you want pity and disgust?

It is your right.

*The MYSTERIOUS STRANGER begins to
cut the MAID. His treatment of her should be
both violent and highly sexual.*

*Elizabeth is at first repulsed.*

ELIZABETH
Even I balked at that.

I'm not a man. That's not how we do things.

But then I realized that I had no man to do those things for me. It was
up to me. It was up to me to fend for myself. To find my own pleasure.
To make my own way.

What choice did I have?

I could have married. I could have moved in with relatives. But where
would that leave me?

Someone else would be the master, and I but the servant — a slave clad
in ermine.

That would not do.

Here, in my own home, I was the mistress.

Here, my word was law.

But an aging woman cannot live alone.

I needed to be young.

I needed to be beautiful again.

*ELIZABETH begins to youthen.*

To be my own mistress, I had to be able to wield power to protect
myself.

The taste. The feel against my skin.

It filled me with fire.

It filled me with strength.

> *The PRIEST looks on, appalled, yet attracted.*

Together, we made me young again.

> *As the number of victims mounts, screaming and writhing....*

PRIEST
And no one noticed the missing girls?

ELIZABETH
Why would they?

Why would they care?

I had plenty of money. I gave them Christian burials. I paid off their families.

I even had local women find me new girls as the supply ran low.

I owned them. What could they do?

I would promise them work. And I'd give them work. I'd make them sew. But I'd make them stand naked in the courtyard to sew. What the weather was did not matter. If they didn't finish their sewing, they would be brought to me for punishment.

Eventually I had a cage built. The bars were covered with spikes. I would burn the girls and make them dance. Then they would bleed.

And I, I had my new love. And I was young.

*The stage becomes washed with blood red.*

What would you do?

There is a story about a young man who was loved by a great goddess. She offered him one gift. He asked for immortality and she gave it him. But he made a mistake. He forgot to ask for eternal youth. And so he grew old and withered. And eventually was of no use to anyone.

I would be the butterfly to his grasshopper.

I would not make the same mistake. Whatever it took.

> *ELIZABETH does a dance of youth for the PRIEST and for the STRANGER. The dance should be strangely erotic, disgusting, passionate and violent at the same time.*
>
> *As she dances, the number of victims mounts.*
>
> *As the dance ends, and the PRIEST looks on horrified, the STRANGER has disappeared.*
>
> *Then COUNT THURZO bursts into the room.*
>
> *The PRIEST prays.*

# SCENE IV

ELIZABETH
You!

THURZO
Yes.

> *Pause.*

ELIZABETH
You'll regret this intrusion, Thurzo.

THURZO
Do you think so?

> *ELIZABETH turns desperately to the STRANGER, but he is gone.*

PRIEST
So, lady, how did you get caught?

ELIZABETH
A simple mistake. It was silly, really.

We'd taken a short trip. But there were several girls for whom we not yet arranged burial. I had them hidden under the bed. In this very room. We'd covered them with lime. To try and hide the smell. Well. It was unseasonably warm those few days. A guest smelled them and went to Count Thurzo.

Finally, he had a reason to call.

PRIEST
Lady?

ELIZABETH
Do you really think anyone cared whether or not I killed a few peasant girls?

PRIEST
As I recall, there were a few minor nobles on your list.

ELIZABETH
Yes, I suppose that the list wasn't a very good idea, at the end of the day.

Anyway, after a couple of hundred....

PRIEST
Six hundred and fifty.

I've seen the list.

ELIZABETH
Very well. Six hundred and fifty.

After 650 girls, a few mistakes are bound to be made.

PRIEST
How can you be so blasé?

ELIZABETH
I don't have your Catholic sensibilities.

PRIEST
Even Protestants object to mass murder.

ELIZABETH
I'm a Lutheran.

Anyway, Count Thurzo had been my enemy for years.

PRIEST
Why?

*Pause.*

ELIZABETH
You could have written and told me you wanted to visit. You might not have needed guards.

THURZO
I'm no longer a rutting child.

And you're no longer so young.

ELIZABETH
No?

But I was young. Curious.

*THURZO slaps Elizabeth.*

THURZO
Don't try any of your tricks on me, bitch.

ELIZABETH
Why are you here?

THURZO
As if you don't know.

*Slaps her again.*

You can't even bother to clean up your unholy mess.

Well, lady. We're tired of trying to pretend nothing is happening here.

I'll see you burn.

ELIZABETH
What have I done wrong?

*Stunned silence.*

PRIEST
What had you done wrong?

ELIZABETH
Exactly.

PRIEST
Six-hundred and fifty girls killed and you had to ask?

ELIZABETH
Most of them were just peasants.

I am the Countess Elizabeth Bathory. They can no more condemn me for killing my own peasants than for cutting down my own trees.

THURZO
How many has it been?

How many?

Have you no heart? No feelings?

Your lands are a wasteland. There are no more girls. Just weeping families.

By God I should kill you now.

> *Draws sword as if to kill her.*

> *She spits in his face. This stops him.*

ELIZABETH
You will do no such thing.

How dare you come onto my property and dictate to me.

THURZO
The crown does not look kindly on those who slaughter its subjects.

ELIZABETH
Look to your own house, Thurzo.

I've seen your dungeons. How many have you tortured and killed, cousin?

*Pause.*

PRIEST
Cousin? You have—

ELIZABETH
Don't be naive, priest. Everyone kills peasants. Late paying taxes, you're beaten. Crop yield too low, you're beaten. Disturb some lord's forest, you're hanged. Object to your daughter being raped, you're killed.

It's practically a national past time.

I just happened to be better than most of the others.

All they get is a moment of pleasure.

I got life.

PRIEST
Many people are cruel, yes.

And, sure, some innocent people get hurt. Or worse. But they don't make their slaughter so complete, so cold, so...calculated.

THURZO
Don't try to justify what you've done.

ELIZABETH
Don't try to justify why you're here.

THURZO
I don't have to.

I'm only here to see that you die.

ELIZABETH
You wouldn't kill me. You love me.

THURZO
You mean nothing to me. You never did. You never could.

ELIZABETH
And what about your son?

THURZO
My son is at home with his family.

ELIZABETH
Not that son, you bastard.

Our son.

*Pause.*

THURZO
What son?

ELIZABETH
Don't you remember?

THURZO
I remember that one night.

ELIZABETH
When you raped me.

THURZO
Is that what you call it?

Well, Cuz, you can't thread a spinning needle.

You were a whore then as you are now.

You were always a little slut. You with your young body, rubbing it against me.

THURZO

I loved you.

THURZO
And you got me.

ELIZABETH
I didn't know.

I didn't know what was—

THURZO
The hell you didn't. You knew exactly what you were doing.

ELIZABETH
I was thirteen.

I had never even been alone with a man before.

And when you came to wish me well that day, all I could remember was the older boy who had been so kind to me when I was a girl.

THURZO
You were a wanton slut.

I wonder what Ferenc must have thought.

ELIZABETH
I couldn't tell him. He would have killed—

> *THURZO slaps ELIZABETH.*

Please, no.

I was to be married.

Is this what you wanted?

Is it?

THURZO
Bitch.

Tell me about the son.

ELIZABETH
We had a child.

PRIEST
You and Thurzo?

I know your history, Lady. I know of no child.

ELIZABETH
He came to me. To wish me well. My dashing cousin. Young, strong.

He embraced me, and then….

> *She remembers the rape. The rape segues into labor.*

I didn't know what was happening at first. I'd never — I didn't.

> *The labor intensifies.*

By the time my mother knew what was happening, it was too late to take care of it.

MOTHER
How could you? You little whore. Think of what this could do to you. To the family. To me.

> *Labor continues.*

After all I did for you. After all the arrangements I made. How stupid could you be?

ELIZABETH
One night I ran away and tried to find Thurzo. I thought that because he'd…that he loved me. I thought he'd marry me.

But they found me the next morning. I had the child that night.

> *ELIZABETH gives birth. Well, sort of.*

Such a beautiful little thing. Small and perfect.

A little me.

A little body. So small.

I don't know how any person could be so small.

MOTHER
Well, now I suppose I'll have to clean up this mess you made for yourself.

I should have married you to a farmer. He would be used to living in the offal.

Give me the child.

ELIZABETH
No! No!

Not my boy!

Not my baby!

MOTHER
Give it to me!

Here, get rid of it. Expose it. Drown it. I do not care. Just get rid of it.

LADY IN WAITING (V.O.)
*[Laughs and giggles]*
Have you seen Ferenc?

He's so handsome.

The Emperor might be coming.

You're so lucky.

*Etcetera.*

ELIZABETH
I got to hold him only for a few minutes. Then he was taken away. He was sent…away.

PRIEST
Where? What happened to the child?

ELIZABETH
Away.

And what did Thurzo care? He'd taken what I could not give him. He'd destroyed beauty and innocence and left, like a general who conquers land to leave it fallow.

He might have me now, but I would use every weapon I could.

THURZO
Where is this child?

ELIZABETH
You would like to know that wouldn't you?

THURZO
Tell me where the boy is.

ELIZABETH
No.

THURZO
I could kill you here and now. No one would blame me.

ELIZABETH
You're going to kill me anyway. Why not now? But, I won't tell you where the boy is.

THURZO
By God you will.

ELIZABETH
I called for you for days. "Come take us away!"

But you never came.

So one night, I crept down to where they were keeping the boy and took him away.

THURZO
Where?

ELIZABETH
Out to the fishpond.

THURZO
No.

ELIZABETH
He was so tiny. I took off his blanket and looked into his little eyes. He kicked and splashed in the water.

THURZO
No.

ELIZABETH
He must have been so cold he struggled so.

THURZO
No.

ELIZABETH
His cries came out as bubbles that splashed onto the cobblestones.

THURZO
No.

ELIZABETH
Finally quiet.

THURZO
No.

ELIZABETH
Finally calm.

THURZO
No.

ELIZABETH
Finally dead!

THURZO
No!

ELIZABETH
You didn't want him, did you?

THURZO
You fiend!

I might have loved you once. But you — you are a beast!

ELIZABETH
A beast?

I am the Countess Elizabeth Bathory.

THURZO
You are a murderer.

ELIZABETH
I am ordained by God.

THURZO
To kill your own son! My son!

ELIZABETH
It was my son! To do with as I pleased!

PRIEST
Your own son?

ELIZABETH
Oh, he was sent off to a distant cousin in Bavaria. He's doing fine.

They were going to kill me anyway. The sooner the better. Besides, our forests are practically carpeted with exposed children. I was surprised he was so upset.

> *Motions. Elizabeth reacts as if her arms are being held out.*

THURZO
I charge you with the slaughter of God's servants and His Majesty's subjects.

> *Begins to lash her.*

ELIZABETH
I am the Countess Elizabeth Bathory.
> *The lashings continue.*

THURZO
As the Palatine Prince of Hungary, I condemn you to death.

ELIZABETH
I am sovereign. I deny your right.

*The lashings continue. As they continue, the screams of ELIZABETH's victims' echo. Added to that are the cries and laments of their families, looking for and mourning their lost daughters.*

THURZO
By my right—

ELIZABETH
I am the Countess Elizabeth Bathory.

THURZO
And in the name of God the Father—

ELIZABETH
My word is law.

THURZO
I condemn you.

ELIZABETH
Then do it.

I won't give you what you really want, so kill me.

THURZO
And for the death of my son—

ELIZABETH
What? You can't kill me twice.

*The lashing stops. THURZO looks at her back and shudders.*

THURZO
—I condemn you to life.

*Long pause.*

ELIZABETH
No.

THURZO.
You, Elizabeth, are like a wild animal.

ELIZABETH
Never.

THURZO
You are in the last months of your life. You do not deserve to breathe
the air on earth, nor to see the light of the Lord.

ELIZABETH
Kill me then.

THURZO
You shall disappear from this world and shall never reappear in it again.

ELIZABETH
You do not have this right.

THURZO
The shadows will envelop you and you will find time to repent your
bestial life.

ELIZABETH
I am the Countess Elizabeth Bathory.

THURZO
I condemn you, Lady, to lifelong imprisonment in your own castle.

ELIZABETH
I demand to stand trial.

THURZO
May you enjoy growing old.

*THURZO leaves through the door. As it is being locked and walled up, we hear the screams and accusations of her VICTIMS and their loved ones.*

*ELIZABETH collapses near the fireplace.*

# SCENE V

ELIZABETH
Three years!

Three years, priest.

Three years alone in this room.

On some days I can hear children playing in the gardens. I can hear lovers laughing. I hear the balls and parties. I smell the flowers.

How I want to feel the grass beneath my feet.

The sun on my face.

*Pause.*

Is that so much to ask for?

When I was a child, things were so much simpler. I lived in a great castle. Surrounded by servants. I was given everything I wanted or needed.

My friends and I would skip and jump through the woods, wade in the streams. Play in the flowers. We would lie on a grassy knoll and let the sun warm us and turn our cheeks red. We would dance in the snow and laugh at the storms.

What did we care about duty? Our duty was to be young and to play. That was no hardship. It was our pleasure.

Is that so much to ask for?

But that all changed.

As a child I became a mother. As a child I became a wife and mistress of a great estate. All of a sudden I had duties, responsibilities. I had a husband, servants, accounts. I was hostess and confidant. I sat and smiled as kings and princes pinched my cheek and congratulated my husband on his new toy.

Where were my toys? Who congratulated me? Where were my friends?

Why wasn't I allowed to be a child forever?

Is that so much to ask?

All I ever wanted was to remain young. To remain beautiful. To have pleasure and joy.

Is that so much to ask for?

I am a woman. That is all that I am. I don't think that's so bad. But I never got to hold my own child. I never really got to be a child. I was never a child to my own mother. I was just an object. A bargaining chip. A deal, an exchange, a commodity.

I just wanted to be loved for who I was. Who I am. What I was. Not because of what I meant. Or was worth.

Is that so much to ask for.

*Pause.*

What do you want, priest?

Don't tell me to save my soul. What do you get out of this?

Advancement?

PRIEST
Confess your sins to God.

ELIZABETH
How old are you, priest? Twenty-five?

Is your career moving too slowly for you?

Will I be able to help you that much?

PRIEST
Confess. Return to God's Grace.

ELIZABETH
Did you know that there have been Popes younger than you?

PRIEST
If you confess, if you leave off your heresy and join the true church, I
might be able to convince the Archbishop to ask that you be allowed into
the garden.

From time to time.

ELIZABETH
What if you could have more time?

PRIEST
You would rather rot here alone?

ELIZABETH
Maybe I could help you.

PRIEST
Repent.

ELIZABETH
Piss on you, priest. I will not be a part of your political games. You will
not have Elizabeth Bathory.

PRIEST
Repent.

In the name of God the father, repent.

ELIZABETH
Would you like me to help you?

PRIEST
Repent.

For your soul.

In the name of Jesus Christ the Son of God, repent.

ELIZABETH
Would you like me to give you more time?

PRIEST
Repent.

For mine!

In the name of the Holy Spirit, repent!

ELIZABETH
Is that why your here?

*Softly we hear the voices of her VICTIMS pleading for mercy. Gradually the voices become louder and louder. Then come the voices of the FAMILIES OF THE VICTIMS crying for there lost daughters. The VICTIMS finally begin to scream as they are tortured. ELIZABETH'S VOICE begins to call out her refrain "I am the Countess Elizabeth Bathory. Ordained by God. I can do know wrong." (Or "My desires are law." Or "Who are you to condemn me?")*

*At some point during this ELIZABETH turns and looks at the PRIEST. He drops to his knees.*

*The voices continue over his speech and the
PRIEST must compete with them and still be
understood. Whether or not he hears the voices is
not for me to decide.*

PRIEST
Save me, O God, by thy name, and by thy might defend my cause. Hear
me, O God, my prayer. Hearken to the words of my mouth. Turn back
the evil upon my foes. In your faithfulness destroy them. Hearken, O
God, to my prayer. Turn not away from my pleading. Give heed to me
and answer me.

*By the time the PRIEST gets to the end, the
voices should be deafening. ELIZABETH has
not moved all this time, but has merely stared at
the PRIEST.*

*All sound abruptly stops.*

PRIEST
What devil are you?

*There is a long and equally deafening silence.*

ELIZABETH
No devil you would ever want to meet.

*Again silence.*

*What follows is the PRIEST's next speech in
toto. Following that will be ELIZABETH's
lines. The two speeches, and her actions, may
overlap to some degree.*

PRIEST
I exorcise thee, most vile spirit, in the name of Jesus Christ.

Hear and fear, seducer of men.

Depart, in the name of the Father, and of the Son, and of the Holy Ghost.

Yield, yield to the minister of Christ. For it is God who commands thee.

God the father commands thee.

God the Son commands thee.

God the Holy Ghost commands thee.

The sacred cross commands thee.

The faith of the holy apostles commands thee.

The blood of the martyrs commands thee.

The word made flesh commands thee.

He who was born of the Virgin commands thee.

Jesus of Nazareth commands thee.

Now depart! Depart, seducer. For if thou hast deceived man, thou canst not mock God.

ELIZABETH
I know what you want, priest.

You want what they all want.

Do you really think that any of them cared about a few hundred peasant girls? There will always be more peasants.

No, they feared me.

There feared what they would do for me.

This face. This is what they wanted to see.

This body. This is what they wanted to touch.

Noble, bishop, king. They all wanted.

And it was mine to give or not.

They could not control me as they wanted to.

That is why they locked me away.

Do you see what they wanted?

Do you understand why they were so scared?

What do you want, priest?

Do you really want me to go?

Do you fear that I will stay?

I am young and beautiful. I will be young and beautiful when these castle walls are dust. When you are dead and forgotten.

You want confession, priest? I have loved more than you could imagine. I have felt their hands on me. Their breath on my skin. They filled me with their life and their need.

I have seen their desire destroy them as it fed me.

*Long pause.*

Touch me, priest.

> *She takes the PRIEST's hands and places them on her.*

Give me your youth and I will give you mine.

Give me your love and I will confess to you.

Love me, Priest. Love me and I will give you all you want.

*She mounts him.*

Take, for this is given to you for everlasting youth.

I entrust to *you*, priest, my whole life and hope.

I believe and, priest, that you are truly the one who came into the world to save me. I also believe that this is truly your pure body and that this is truly your precious blood. Therefore, I pray to you, have mercy upon me, and forgive my transgressions, voluntary involuntary, in word and deed, known and unknown. And make me worthy without condemnation to partake of your pure Mysteries life eternal.

Take, for this is the salvation of your servant, gracious and bountiful and long suffering, who desires not death but rather that she live.

> *With a scream, the PRIEST struggles and fights his way from ELIZABETH.*
>
> *She collapses into his arms. They lie spent for a long moment. Slowly he rolls ELIZABETH from him. She ends up near the fireplace, just as she was at the beginning of the play. He takes the ragged cloak from the floor and covers her completely with it.*
>
> *Emotionally, spiritually, and physically spent, he drops to his knees and prays silently. Finished, he crosses himself.*

ELIZABETH
Father.

PRIEST
No.

No!

ELIZABETH
You want me.

PRIEST
Yes.

No!

*Long pause.*

ELIZABETH
Men have killed for what I would give you.

PRIEST
And they will burn in hell.

ELIZABETH
I am beautiful.

PRIEST
Yes.

No.

No!

ELIZABETH
I am beauty.

PRIEST
You are not.

ELIZABETH
I have the power. Yield to me.

Yield to me!

PRIEST
I deny you.

I deny your power.

This is not beauty. This is only flesh.

Whatever you may have been, you are nothing now.

> *They look at each other for some moments.*

Guard!

Guard!

Open the door.

> *After a moment, the locks are removed and the door opened. The GUARD enters.*

I am ready to go. My job is finished.

GUARD
Yes, father.

Is she?

PRIEST
Leave her!

GUARD
Sir?

PRIEST
Let her remain here.

Seal the door again.

GUARD
May I look at her, father?

PRIEST
No.

GUARD
It's only that, well, she was supposed to be so lovely.

PRIEST
Her sins have caught up with her.

Beauty, my son, comes from God. It is a gift for him to give or take away.

Salvation lies in faith and good deeds. Therein lies true beauty.

When she approaches God's judgment, she will wear her true face.

Let us leave this foul place.

*The two leave.*

*As we hear the locks being replaced and the door being walled up again, all we see is the lonely figure or ELIZABETH.*

*The lights fade.*

# *About the Author*

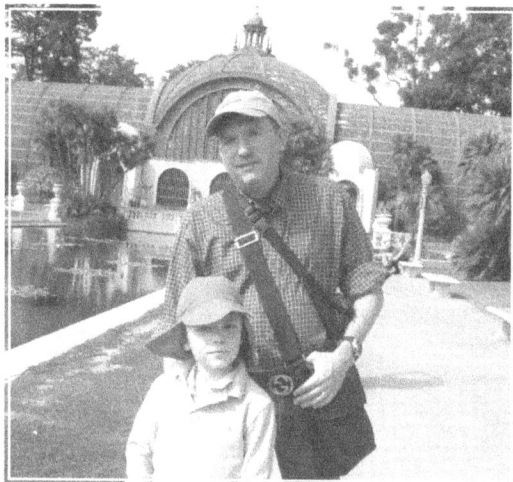

*The Author and his son, Christopher*

Edward Eaton has studied and taught at many schools in the States, China, Israel, Oman, and France. He holds a PhD is Theatre History and Literature and has worked extensively as a theatre director and fight choreographer. As a writer, he has been a newspaper columnist, a theatre critic, and has published and presented many scholarly papers. He is author of the young adult series *Rosi's Doors*, including: Rosi's Castle, Rosi's Time, and Rosi's Company. Other publications include the plays Orpheus and Eurydice and Elizabeth Bathory. In addition to his academic and creative pursuits, Ted is an avid SCUBA diver and skier. He currently lives and works in Boston, Massachusetts with his wife Silviya, a hospital administrator, and his son Christopher.